Holding Fast

Jews Respond to American Gun Violence

Edited by Rabbi Menachem Creditor

Holding Fast
Jews Respond to American Gun Violence

All rights reserved. No part of this book may be reproduced or transmitted in any form or by means electronic or mechanical, including photocopying, recording, or by any information storage and retrieval system, without permission in writing from the author.

2018 Paperback Edition, *First Printing*

Cover Image: "*Tree of Life*," created by students, family, and friends in honor of the 18th anniversary of the Solomon Schechter School of Manhattan, NY

Copyright © 2018 Menachem Creditor
Cover Art © 2018 Solomon Schechter School
of Manhattan, NY

All rights reserved.
ISBN: 9781790532872

Holding Fast

"She [Torah] is a Tree of Life
to all who hold fast to her,
and those who support Her are content;
Her ways are ways of pleasantness,
and all Her paths are peace."

Proverbs 3:17-18

In memory of:

Joyce Fienberg *z"l*
Richard Gottfried *z"l*
Rose Mallinger *z"l*
Jerry Rabinowitz *z"l*
Cecil Rosenthal *z"l*,
David Rosenthal *z"l*
Bernice Simon *z"l*
Sylvan Simon *z"l*
Daniel Stein *z"l*
Melvin Wax *z"l*
Irving Younger *z"l*

also by Menachem Creditor

(*ed.*) To Banish Darkness: *Modern Reflections on Hanukkah*

yes, my child: *poems*

Intense Beginnings: *Selected Writings, 2014*

What Does it Mean? *Selected Writings 2006-2013*

(*ed.*) Not By Might: *Channeling the power of Faith to End Gun Violence*

And Yet We Love: *Poems*

Primal Prayers: *Spiritual Responses to a Real World*

(*ed.*) The Hope: *American Jewish Voices in Support of Israel*

Commanded to Live: *One Rabbi's Reflections on Gun Violence*

Siddur Tov LeHodot: *Shabbat Morning Transliterated Prayerbook*

(*ed.*) Thanksgiving Torah: *Jewish Reflections on an American Holiday*

(*ed.*) A Manifesto for the Future: *Conservative/Masorti Judaism Dreaming from Within*

(*ed.*) Peace in Our Cities: *Rabbis Against Gun Violence*

Slavery, Freedom, and Everything Between: *The Why, How and What of Passover;* co-edited with Rabbi Aaron Alexander

A Pesach Rhyme

Avodah: A Yom Kippur Story

Rabbi Rebecca and the Thanksgiving Leftovers

A portion of the proceeds from this book will support efforts to end the American Gun Violence epidemic.

CONTENTS

9	**Introduction** Rabbi Menachem Creditor	
13	**To the Man Who Tried to Kill Me** Orelle Magnani	
15	**After Parkland, I Said, "It Could've been me.' Now it is.** Ada Perlman	
21	**Shepherding a Jewish Community through a Mass Shooting** Rabbi Amy Bardack	
27	**Profiles** Audrey N. Glickman	
33	**If Not Now When, If Not Together, then Never** Rabbi Jeremy Weisblatt and Chris Harrison	
39	**Before the Synagogue Shooting** Rosanne Levine	
43	**A Letter to Baby Frankie** Rabbi Jodie Gordon	
47	**Breast Cancer and Firearms Mortality** Sabina Robinson, PhD	
53	**How to End Gun Violence: Organize** Yael Perlman	
59	**Remarks at a Boston Vigil in Solidarity with the Tree of Life Synagogue** Rabbi David Lerner	
65	**After Pittsburgh, We Must Remember** Rabbi Menachem Creditor	

69	**The Blood of the Children Cries Out from the Ground!** Rabbi Gary S. Creditor
75	**Looking Evil in the Eye** Rabbi Joshua Hammerman
81	**Anti-Semitism and Anti-Black Racism Both Advance White Supremacy** Jeanné Isler and Timi Gerson
87	**Sermon for Solidarity Shabbat after the Pittsburgh Tragedy** Rabbi Joseph R. Black
95	**A Prophetic Response to Gun Violence** Rabbi Menachem Creditor
103	**Targets** Lisa Rappaport
109	**A Prayer for One Who Enters a Synagogue** Rabbi Jill Zimmerman
113	**Prayer after Tragedy: Hashkiveinu** Rabbi David Paskin
115	**Where God Is** Stacey Zisook Robinson
117	**The Courage to Press Forward** Rabbi Shawn Israel Zevit
119	**A Tree of Life** Rabbi Ben Herman
121	**Afterword: Why Pittsburgh Matters** Rabbi Jeff Salkin

Jews Respond to American Gun Violence

INTRODUCTION

I have never edited a book such as this and hope to never again.

On October 27, 2018, a domestic terrorist murdered 11 Jews during Shabbat services at the Tree of Life Synagogue in Pittsburgh. This was both the worst Anti-Semitic attack in America's history and the 12th shooting massacre at an American house of worship in 3 years. Too much blood has spilled, killing upwards of 30,000 Americans every year. The Pittsburgh Shooting Massacre was both Jewish trauma and American blasphemy.

The voices assembled in this collection - teens, rabbis, and others - reflect a particular Jewish experience of hatred as well as the understanding that the United States of America is in the midst of a Gun Violence epidemic that violates both sanctuary and street. I have been ravaged and inspired, sometimes in the same moment, reviewing the responses, essays, and poems that comprise this holy collection, and important contribution to the growing corpus of American writing engaged in the fight for more than 30,000 lives each and every year.

It has been an intense and humbling experience to collect these voices. It is a holy obligation upon us all to hear their painful, clarion collective call.

Every time the Torah is read, Jews chant "*She [Torah] is a Tree of Life to all who hold fast to her* (Proverbs 3:17)"

We, fellow ravaged American citizens, must hold fast to each other as we cry out for more than the necessary healing.

We demand an end to the ongoing Gun Violence Epidemic plaguing our nation.

Rabbi Menachem Creditor
December, 2018 / Tevet 5779

Speech has tremendous power. If you know how, you can even whisper to a gun so that it cannot shoot.

> Rabbi Nachman of Breslov
> *Likutei Moharan II, 96*

To the Man Who Tried to Kill Me
Orelle Magnani

*Orelle Magnani is 15 years old.
She lives in Squirrel Hill.*

To the Man Who Tried to Kill Me,

On October twenty seventh you broke me. You made me weak, shocked, and numb.

You found pride in hurting me. You found joy in shooting eighteen people in a place I once thought was undoubtedly safe. *Tree of Life*. A place I have been to countless times. A place I considered one of my synagogues, and most importantly, a place I found peace in.

But on a typical, rainy Saturday morning you took that all away from me. You parked your car in the same place I did every Wednesday morning of seventh grade. You followed my footsteps and entered the building.

But instead of nonchalantly wandering in with a backpack, you walked in with a loaded AR-15 and two handguns. Instead of greeting your friends and saying good morning to the seniors, you screamed "all these Jews need to die" at three innocent congregations. Instead of turning left and entering the service quietly, you shot through the glass door and raided the sanctuary.

Within minutes you killed eleven people, and you weren't finished. You were on your way to the next synagogue. *My synagogue.*

You had another loaded AR-15 waiting in your green Chevy ready to kill me. Ready to kill my mom, ready to kill my dad, and ready to kill my whole community.

But you didn't make it. The first responders beat you to it. You were shot within seconds. If they had been a minute late I could be dead. My friends could be dead. My world could be dead.

I pray the worst for you, but what you did won't stop me. I will mourn. But most importantly, I will remember. May their memories be a blessing, and may you learn that resorting to violence is never the answer.

Sincerely,
Orelle Magnani

After Parkland, I said, 'It could've been me.' Now it is.
Ada Perlman

> *Ada Perlman is a freshman at The Ellis School in Pittsburgh, Pennsylvania. She is an active member in her school's theater community, and some of her passions include singing and writing. In her summers, she attends camp and travels.*

"*What?*" I heard my mother's disbelief from my bedroom. It was about 10:15 on October 27th. I disregarded the nervousness in her voice and went back to sleep.

A few moments later, she came into my room and sat on my bed. She was solemn and sober and I could not figure out why. "Ada." She said with loss in her voice. "Abba is okay, but there was a shooting at Tree of Life."

A shooting? In Squirrel Hill? At my shul?

That is impossible. I pinched myself to make sure I was not dreaming, as I had just woken up.

I sprang up in bed. "What? Where is Abba? Is he okay?" I asked, in shock. "He is upstairs," my mother assured me. I sprinted up the stairs faster than I've ever run before and to my relief, there was my dad. I hugged him and squeezed him tight. "I love you. I am so glad you are here." I was still shocked. My dad had his phone out, something that is normally forbidden on Shabbat. He was scrolling through his contacts to see if he could get in touch with any of his congregants or their spouses that were at the shul that day. One picked up. It was the wife of someone who was at shul that day.

"Rabbi, Rabbi! I do not know where he is! Rabbi, I do not know what to do!" The woman's voice was completely hysterical, her tone something I will never forget. My dad tried to reassure the woman that the gunman probably did not go down into our sanctuary, which is in the basement. He was traumatized too, but he had to be a support rock for the others in his congregation. The calls continued, as he got news that two of our congregants were able to get out as well. One of them said he saw someone from our congregation being shot. The man had been hidden in the storage closet with the other three (my father included), but when the gunshots stopped, he thought it was safe to come out.

"They got Mel!!" A frantic voice screamed on the phone. I started crying fearing for my shul, for my future, for my religion, for my city. Will the gunman go to the other shuls? What if he is not acting alone? Will people be afraid to come to shul? Will my dad lose his job because no one will want to come anymore? What about Dan and Rich? Are they alive? So many thoughts buzzed through my head, as I tried to make sense of this terror.

"Come on. Go get dressed. Let us daven." My mother walked with me downstairs to my bedroom as I cried. When I came in, I saw a sign on my wall that I had held up for my school's walkout for the Parkland shooting months before. The sign stated *"It Could Have Been Me."* I burst into tears because the sign was true. Although, I tried to prevent this from happening by protesting and preparing walkouts, my government did not change. It did not change and my congregants became victims of gun violence. My community would be added to the list. The list of all the cities affected by gun violence.

I quickly put on a dress and headed downstairs, eager to daven and ask God to have mercy. I put on my tallis, something I do not usually wear as I'm praying, but I felt the need to create a closer connection to God. My father, my mother, and I put on our prayer shawls and opened our siddurim as we began to pray.

> *"Elohai neshama, she-natata bi, tehora hi — the soul that You, my God, have given me is pure."*

We repeated this, as we cried in disbelief and shock. At every word the phone rang or there was a knock at the door. This was real. *Our little synagogue in Squirrel Hill.* Neighbors came to the door and family members called updating us on the situation because we had not been checking the news. Some came in tears, relieved that we were okay.

The rest of that afternoon was a blur. Visitors came all day, and news stations had even started calling us. We had gotten the news that three of our congregants were dead. It was surreal. At night, we went to the JCC to comfort the families of the victims. I felt so important entering that building because only certain people were allowed in. When we entered, everyone was silent, hugging each other, and trying to make sense of it all.

I talked to Rabbi Jeffrey Myers who was someone that gave me a lot of hope. "We can't let this stop us" he said firmly. "We need to keep going and show everyone who Jews really are."

He was exactly right and that is what got me through the week of funerals, shivas, and mourning. Our city of bridges lifted each other up, survivor or not survivor, Jew or non-Jew, we were all there for each other.

Yes, it was me. A not-so-average 14-year-old girl. But now I am different. The city I have lived in most of my life is now defined by the violence that took place there. No one else should have to endure any of the effects of this kind of violence.

Enough is enough.

Jews Respond to American Gun Violence

Shepherding a Jewish Community through a Mass Shooting[1]
Rabbi Amy Bardack

> *Rabbi Amy Bardack is the director of Jewish life and learning at the Jewish Federation of Greater Pittsburgh and resides in Squirrel Hill..*

I could write a book on how to guide a Jewish community in the aftermath of a mass shooting. I pray that no one will have to read it. But given the rise in anti-Semitic hate crimes, your town might be next. So let me help you.

I am a rabbi at the Jewish Federation of Greater Pittsburgh. Our job, in normal times, is to assess the needs of the community and determine how to meet those needs. It is because of the way we worked and the networks we created before the massacre, in the Jewish community and in the

---

[1] the piece originally appeared in eJewishPhilanthropy.com on November 12, 2018 and appears here with the permission of the author and EJP.

city as a whole, that we were able to care for our community after it.

We mobilized an initial response to the shooting in one hour. Next, the staff divided up responsibilities. First came supporting the victims and their families; then, serving the community. "I'm on rabbis and educators," I volunteered. There was no road map to follow. We rolled up our sleeves and went to work. Here's what I've learned so far.

Invest in Relationships:

Two years ago, I spent the first three months in my job meeting with everyone in the community. It sometimes felt frivolous. But in this time of crisis, I needed those relationships. "Let's huddle and strategize," said my Orthodox male colleague in his black coat and hat, standing next to me at a funeral. "Here's who I'm hearing needs help," said the Cohenet, a feminist spiritual leader. Pittsburgh is known as a community where Jews of different stripes talk to each other and work together. That is not the case in other cities I've lived in. After the Boston marathon bombings, a team of disaster-trained chaplains was unable to convene a meeting of rabbis. I've convened three meetings thus far, all widely attended. Because of the way we've always worked together across denominational lines, we were able to collaborate in an atmosphere of mutual trust in the wake of a massacre.

Work with Partners:

We were fortunate to be able to mobilize an initial response within one hour of the shooting because we already had strong partnership with two communal agencies: the Jewish Community Center and Jewish Family and Community Services. We worked hand in glove with those organizations, alongside the American Red Cross and the FBI, to create a crisis center immediately. Our community security director at the Federation had already forged strong ties to local and federal law enforcement, which made creating a security plan in the aftermath both smooth and speedy. Our Community Relations Council had well-established relationships with clergy of other faiths, local and state government, and other minority communities. That meant that vigils, rallies, and interfaith services were coordinated within 24 hours. All these partnerships, built in times of peace, were crucial in the aftermath of the shooting.

Teach People How to Help:

We were flooded with offers of help from throughout the world. It was wonderful to hear that others cared, to be enveloped by people of all faiths, near and far. But many of the offers were not helpful. Some asked us to provide personalized service like itineraries and customized maps of the area so they could provide what they hoped would be support.

Others wanted us to organize a public lecture for them to share their wisdom with us. At an emergency clergy meeting, we all agreed: We're going to say no. No to the busloads of young people who needed us to provide housing and food. No to the self-proclaimed mental health gurus who thought they alone had the skills to heal us. "Unless you have low ego, high emotional intelligence, and unique expertise, we cannot welcome you now," became my stock response. My advice for potential helpers: be humble, don't create more work for us, do what we ask you to do, and don't be offended when we say no.

Support the Jewish Professionals:

Rabbis and Jewish professionals were ourselves traumatized, not just caretakers of those who were. In order to take care of others, we needed to take care of ourselves. We relied on our network of national rabbinical and chaplaincy associations to bring in rabbis to provide pastoral care to clergy and to extend our reach to those who wanted to speak with a rabbi. We used our connections to the Pittsburgh medical community to deploy trauma specialists to help Jewish professionals both care for themselves and understand the many reactions they were seeing in others. Chaplains also helped Jewish leaders supervise their employees who were traumatized, and guided us in striking the right tone when it was time for some of us to begin to return to regular business.

Give a Message that We Are Moving Forward Together:

Our Israeli brothers and sisters knew terror well, and they had unmatched expertise. The Israel Trauma Coalition, which helps communities around the world manage these kinds of attacks, sent a delegation of five experts. They met with rabbis and educators, helping us craft the right message and tone that would help promote healing. They helped parents and children understand the symptoms of acute traumatic response. Our message, they advised, needed to be that we can make a choice to move forward as Jews together.

Pittsburgh is a resilient city, the Steel City. We have always known how to move forward. And we will again, serving as a model for the profound strength of pluralistic community-building for Jewish communities everywhere.

Jews Respond to American Gun Violence

Profiles

Audrey N. Glickman

> *Audrey N. Glickman is a member of Tree of Life Congregation and works as Rabbi's Assistant at Congregation Beth Shalom. Her careers have spanned theatrical production, advertising, legal secretarial, and political/governmental work, including four years serving as chief of staff to an elected official. And she is honored occasionally to lead Shabbat Pesukei DeZimra.*

Since this past summer, with each Mourner's Kaddish I've remembered Antwon Rose II, a 17-year-old friend of an acquaintance of my son, who was shot dead by a police officer in the borough of East Pittsburgh on June 19, 2018. Considered a smart, kind, gentle and generous individual, Antwon was killed apparently without a second thought as he ran from a jitney stopped for another passenger. He was shot in the back. Profiled.

The good folks of the *Tree of Life*, *Dor Hadash*, and *New Light* congregations were also shot apparently without a second thought, murdered in the middle of prayers, murdered for our religion itself. Remembered as sweet, funny, caring, smart, kind, gentle and generous individuals, they were each the very definition of good people. Profiled.

We Jews teach our children that in every generation there will be people against us, there will be hatred that we must endure. We have done this for thousands of years. Of course, we are not the only ones teaching our families to be prepared, telling them that someone is going to hate them. Sadly there also are others enduring and addressing this need. We should have found a cure for prejudice by now; we are the ones with the longest experience.

We repeat often enough, to ourselves and to others, that we are responsible for teaching the values of light, love, knowledge, and compassion.

There is no way to know who next will learn to hate, who will be led from positive thoughts to negative. We cannot know who will take someone's conspiracy theory and conflate it into a threat that must be annihilated. There is no way to surmise who doesn't know any better, who has been deluded into hatred, and who is seriously in need of mental health attention or confinement. It is impossible to understand the motivation, and we cannot control it.

Perhaps we can control the instigations and the access to implements of death. And with common sense management of the common good, we can help assure that those who need medical attention of any sort can get it. And of course, we can work to educate the general public about the value of every single individual life.

Positive must overcome negative. We must take hold of our society and collectively steer it toward the benefit of all. We have to be inclusive. And we have to model the behavior ourselves.

We must stop being divisive, making horrible jokes with common stereotypes, decreeing people to be not good enough, grouping people into categories and making assumptions, accusing others of causing the ills of the world without facts and without reason to condemn. And we have to stop giving platforms to those who instigate this behavior especially when disguising it as "politics" or "entertainment." Or "religion."

The Tree of Life in Pittsburgh is my shul, I am a member. We are a congregation with deep roots, warmth, compassion, a zest for discussion and learning, and a history of social action, of assisting those in need. We are a congregation filled with light and love, a congregation that began before the Civil War.

I was there on October 27th. I felt that hatred in the air, like an act of war the gunshots rang out down the hallway and our friends were murdered. We were saying the Kaddish D'Rabbanan when the murder began. The Kaddish D'Rabbanan is also a Mourner's Kaddish.

Prejudice, discrimination, stereotyping, profiling, hatred, violence, murder: all are wrong, regardless the target. We Jews are accustomed to enduring and surviving, and going on to live. But we have to be better at arresting the malignancy before it begins, against anyone. And we have to be wary that we are not guilty ourselves.

First responders from across the region working together collectively stopped the murdering on that day, kept the shooter from possibly going to other congregations. There were dozens of public safety personnel who rushed toward the danger, who got the injured out and to the hospital, who ultimately brought the shooter out of the building. There is a police officer still in the hospital over a month later.

The response we saw in Pittsburgh should be the way of the world: the entire city gathered around us, held us up, took care of us, showed solidarity, treated us as the friends we hope we are to all of them. Our city has no place for negative feelings and nefarious actions, we live on love and we enjoy each other.

We intend to rebuild and strengthen the Tree of Life. There is a lot of internal damage to the building, and there are a lot of measures we must take for increased security, as sad as that thought is. Yet every minute we are not yet back inside our building, in our praying spaces, classrooms, offices, and gathering areas, is a further victimization. And we do not want to continue to be "victims" or "survivors." We have lives to lead and a world to repair. In the memory of those whom we lost, whom we loved, we have a lot of improvement to accomplish.

We are humbly and immeasurably grateful for the outstretched arms that have held us and helped us to stand. Let us all lock our hands together now and go forward and make a difference. *Life depends upon it.*

Jews Respond to American Gun Violence

If Not Now When, If Not Together, then Never

Rabbi Jeremy Weisblatt and Chris Harrison

> *Rabbi Jeremy Weisblatt serves as the rabbi of Temple Ohav Shalom in Allison Park, PA and is concurrently in a doctoral program at HUC-JIR, with a focus on Talmud, Responsa and Jewish liturgy. Chris Harrison is a staff member at the Audacious Hospitality arm of the Union for Reform Judaism.*

And the voice of your brother's blood cries out to me...October 27th, 2018, forever seared into my memory, into my soul, has become my clarion call, for the work towards a bloodless tomorrow. The roots for my activism, however, began far earlier. It was the summer of 1995, and I was helping my mother to clean out the car after the sudden death of my father, Rabbi Jeffrey Weisblatt. I stumbled upon the notes for his Yom Kippur sermon for 1995. The topic? The gun violence epidemic in America, and on the cover of his notes was a picture of a handgun, and a lifeless body - images I have never forgotten, images that laid the roots for my eventual activism.

Moving to Chicago in late 2015, I found myself living in a city that for far too long has known the terrible power of loss that can come at the end of the barrel of a gun. With my colleagues of varied faiths and backgrounds, we stood in protest until the community's voices were heard - why was there no trauma center to treat those at the heart of the violence? Those who lived removed from the community, ironically, were the ones with the power to bring change, and they eventually heard the blood of the victims calling from the stained pavements and decided to build hope in the place of pain. Lives were now going to be saved, but only after the bullet left the gun.

Fast forward. Move past Vegas, Parkland, and arrive in October 2018, in Pittsburgh, where the loss of eleven beautiful souls bookended another year of loss. Another year of our brother's blood spilled for no reason, with barely a change in our laws and society. Even after some of the worst acts of gun violence in our country's history, the needle for change still failed to move.

Then came Pittsburgh, and with Pittsburgh, an act of anti-Semitism, an act of terrorism, an act that struck a diverse community to its core, is starting a change in our local community. A change in Pittsburgh is being felt, and needs to spread. It is also a call to see that our country is still failing to speak to the ravages of the gun epidemic plaguing our cities, the loss of lives Americans of Color, and the inherent racism that continues to cut down lives so needlessly of African-Americans.

As this change spreads, and captures our hearts and minds, if it is to last, it means bringing lasting change. How do we do this? We do this by giving voices to those whose lives are as shattered as they are here in Pittsburgh, but who have not been given a voice, and a hope for a better tomorrow. It means having conversations and actions about the entire system - from wanton violence, to mental health, to the racism that costs far too high a price of Americans of Color. Our brother's blood cries out to us - our brother's blood is our fellow human being. As Dr. King tried to teach us, neighbor, is not a geographic term, but is a moral term. It is a moral imperative to prevent the cries of our brother's blood.

When I think of the horror that wanton gun violence has wrought across this country, I don't just think about the countless lives lost that could have been easily prevented through effective legislative measures. I think about the innocent people of color who have been and will be affected by our obsession.

After Pittsburgh, it seemed like the entire American Jewish community was in a state of panic and distress. The immediate response by some well-meaning Jews was to demand armed guards in every synagogue and every Jewish institution. I saw these literal calls for arms on my Facebook news feed and from the mouths of Jews during a roundtable discussion at a Saturday morning Shabbat service, and during each of these occurrences, I felt ignored.

As a Jew of Color, when I hear white Jews demand armed guards or increased security presence in our institutions, it feels like they are ignoring the numerous times that unarmed people of color have been killed extrajudicially for no reason, as well as the many Jews of Color who attend these institutions with increased anxiety because of this new presence. History shows that Jews of Color have often been ignored in these spaces anyway; this time, the stakes just feel much higher.

This issue does not just relate to Jews of Color, but rather people of color as a whole. I can't help but think about the armed black guards that may be serving our communities. I think about Jemel Roberson, an armed security guard who was shot and killed by police after stopping a gunman at a bar in Illinois. I think about EJ

Bradford, Jr., a veteran who was also shot and killed by police for attempting to stop a shooting at a mall in Alabama. Imagine the devastation if, God forbid, a Jewish institution suffered another attack and a police officer arrived at the scene and mistook the man hired to protect the congregants as the culprit.

I must clarify that I am absolutely not anti-law enforcement and I am not against the protection of our synagogues and institutions. I am, however, suggesting that deciding to bring in armed security or police is not something that should be decided quickly or taken lightly. If we are to bring in this extra presence, we must view this decision from every possible angle. We must take the opinions and trepidations of our members of color into consideration during every step. We must ensure that our institutions remain welcoming for all, and that trained greeters ideally accompany whomever we may decide to hire as armed security. I want every last Jew to feel safe among their congregations, including those most marginalized and targeted by gun violence, and I would hope that others in our sacred community would agree.

Jews Respond to American Gun Violence

Before the Synagogue Shooting
Rosanne Levine

> *Rosanne Levine is a Squirrel Hill resident and a member of both Tree of Life and Beth Shalom. She practices as a Nurse Practitioner and has been involved in many community activities as a volunteer. She is eternally grateful for the outpouring of support from the community and the world after this tragic event.*

On October 27, a gunman shot his way into the synagogue that I regularly attend, massacring eleven, physically wounding eight, and emotionally wounding countless individuals. Had I not been scheduled to work as a Nurse Practitioner in clinic that morning, I would have been there and I have a clear picture in my mind of where all of the victims would have been sitting, where I would have been sitting with my father, how I would not have been able to get my father or myself to safety.

But that is not the first, or the last thing to happen in this chain of events.

Before the synagogue shooting, and after, our President engaged in rhetoric that dehumanized, vilified, and denigrated our fellow human beings. That rhetoric, coming from the highest level of government, inspires those who engage in hate groups and hate crimes. We have seen this many times before in our collective history and in my personal family history and, time and again, this vicious speech leads to violent and hateful acts.

Before the synagogue shooting, in 2004, an assault weapons ban was allowed to sunset and the semiautomatic weapon legally bought by this gunman was again allowed to be manufactured and sold. Before the synagogue shooting, in 2013, a bill introduced by Senator Diane Feinstein to again ban assault weapons was defeated in the Senate.

Before the synagogue shooting, the gun industry gave millions of dollars to the NRA, which in turn gave millions of dollars to support candidates, to make "independent expenditures", and to conduct federal lobbying to protect the special interests of an industry that values profits over lives.

Before the synagogue shooting, a Supreme Court decision allowed corporations such as gun industry special interests to make unlimited contributions to PACs and to make

Holding Fast

"independent political expenditures" that support their agendas and their profits.

Before the synagogue shooting, the framers of the U.S. Constitution, who could not have anticipated the invention of assault weapons, wrote these words: "A well-regulated Militia, being necessary to the security of a free State, the right of the people to keep and bear Arms, shall not be infringed." And, somehow our population allowed these words, which clearly refer to the right of the state to have a militia, to be reinterpreted as the right for anyone to manufacture, sell, buy and own assault weapons that have no peacetime use but that wreak tragedy and remove the right to life from countless individuals.

Before the synagogue shooting, the gunman was allowed to remain isolated and unconnected, until he found acceptance in the form of a hate group.

Before the synagogue shooting, Gab.com was allowed to become the home for hatemongering and inciting speech.

Before the synagogue shooting, there were 306 mass shootings involving four or more victims in the U.S. THIS YEAR. After the synagogue shooting, another mass shooting occurred in Thousand Oaks, CA.

Yes, this gunman bears responsibility for his behavior. But it falls to all of us to do everything in our power to look hard at the antecedents and to break the chain of events and thus prevent such a tragedy from ever happening again. Please, demand better from your representatives, senators, and other policy-makers. Hate speech must stop. An assault weapons ban must be introduced and passed. Isolated individuals must be connected during childhood to a society where they can engage in love, not hate.

A Letter to Baby Frankie
Rabbi Jodie Gordon

> *Rabbi Jodie Gordon is a rabbi, educator, and mama who lives in the Berkshires with her husband Josh Bloom, and their daughters Lola and Goldie. She serves Hevreh of Southern Berkshire, an amazing congregation in Great Barrington, MA and is passionate about education, feminism, and Jewish ritual.*

Just about a year ago, I arrived in Pittsburgh for the second time in my life. I have to admit, that if your mother, my best friend, hadn't moved there five years ago, I'm not sure I would have ever made it there. I was there to bless you; to celebrate your arrival in the world by pronouncing your Hebrew name out loud for the first time. I was there to help welcome you into the promise of a covenantal community, by placing the heavy wooden scroll of our Torah in your hands, and by lifting the same tablecloth that served as your parents' wedding chuppah up over you, your sister and parents, as a symbol of blessing and protection.

That morning, your parents gave you the name *"Penina Eden"*. It's a name I wonder if you might now share with your entire Pittsburgh community. It seems that they will need you now, more than ever, and sooner than your young age might suggest, to be a source of hope and strength.

Penina Eden is a name to wear like beautiful armor. Penina, meaning "pearl" reminds us that precious beauty can be formed under pressure and adversity; this seems to be a handy lesson for the moment we're living in. Eden reminds us of a better, more perfect world. Like that idyllic garden, millions of people around the world are praying that Pittsburgh might find its way back to Eden.

Over the last few days, I have listened to interviews with people who have lived in Pittsburgh for generations. To a person, they all remark on how unique a community it is, with connections that are separated by a "a degree and a half" at best, rather than the usual six. What stands out to me, is the palpable sense that this a community with deep roots, and long branches; a community that people come home to. If that's not Eden, I don't know what is.

What was remarkable about that day was about so much more than the personal ties that bind you and me together, Frankie. What was remarkable about that day, was how your

Pittsburgh community showed up, and shared in the blessing. That morning in the chapel that was just down the stairs from your big sister's nursery school classroom, you were surrounded by people who had enfolded your family into the Pittsburgh Jewish community. They offered you this blessing:

> *"Frankie Alice, you are the latest chapter in the unfolding of our lives as a community. You are brand new, a symbol of today and of tomorrow. You are a bridge over which we who welcome you can gaze from this day into future days, from our generation into your generation. You are the newest link in the endless chain of our people's history."*

We made you a lot of promises that day: to surround you with love and protection, so that you can grow up to be a person of substance. In the moments since Saturday's horrific act of terror, I have feared that have already failed you.

And then I remember the words of another famous Yinzer (if I may be so bold as to use that name!). The words of Fred Rogers echo through my mind, reminding us to "look for the helpers." And so, we'll look to the helpers, and even more importantly, we'll look to you, and your sister.

I hope and pray that your Pittsburgh community feels all of us, around the world, holding you all up right now. I know how seriously they took that blessing that day, and I know that even in this time of unimaginable adversity, there will be pearls of blessing and sweetness that helps bring you back, closer to the Eden of that remarkable city.

Breast Cancer and Firearms Mortality
Sabina Robinson, PhD

> *Sabina Robinson earned her PhD in Pharmacology and Experimental Therapeutics from The Johns Hopkins University School of Medicine, and is currently employed as a Research Administrator and Scientific Writer at UPMC Hillman Cancer in Pittsburgh PA. She lives with her husband in the Pittsburgh neighborhood Squirrel Hill, in a home that shares a backyard fence with Tree of Life -- the synagogue where a hate-filled shooter killed one of her friends and 10 other members of the Pittsburgh Jewish Community on the Shabbat morning of October 27, 2018. world after this tragic event.*

According to the U.S. Centers for Disease Control and Prevention, 41,952 Americans died from breast cancer in 2016[2], the most recent year for which accurate data are currently available. For whatever reason, God who created the heavens and earth and all living things, also created misguided cells that are so intent in their quest to "*choose life,*" that they snuff out the lives

---

[2]Deaths: Final Data for 2016. X. Jiaquan, S.L. Murphy, K.D. Kochanek, B. Bastian, and E. Arias. *National Vital Statistics Reports*. Volume 67, Number 5, July 26, 2018.

of the women (mainly) and men (some) in whose bodies they thrive.

And we, as a nation, are truly pissed about it.

So pissed that many of our brightest and most creative minds have dedicated their entire adult lives to trying to solve the problem.

So pissed that tens of thousands of otherwise non-athletic Americans participate in Susan G. Komen *Race for the Cure*™ 5K runs each year and NFL players don pink cleats for October's Breast Cancer Awareness Month.

Pissed to the point where even a divided and dysfunctional Congress can agree that solving the problem is an endeavor worthy of U.S. taxpayer dollars, with $519.9 million spent by the National Cancer Institute[3] and another $91.7 million spent by the Department of Defense[4] on breast cancer research in fiscal year 2016.

Although early detection and new therapeutic strategies have led to improved disease-free and overall breast cancer survival rates over recent decades, the problem of breast cancer-induced mortality is still unsolvable, and the hard work and spending continue.

---

[3] NCI Research Dollars by Cancer, FY 2017 - National Cancer Institute.
[4] Calculated from awards data found for the FY 2016 Congressional Directed Medical Research Program Breast Cancer Research Program at https://cdmrp.army.mil/search.aspx.

Holding Fast

According to U.S. Centers for Disease Control and Prevention, there were 38,658 U.S. firearm deaths in 2016[1]- a number nearly as high the number of people who died of breast cancer. And those of us who are pissed are told that we cannot do anything about it, because there is a Second Amendment. And because this Second Amendment is considered inviolable, no federal dollars have been directed toward studying gun violence, and no real controls have been placed on who can own a gun, or how many guns, or what type of guns. How can this be?

In Torah study fashion, let's go back to the confusing language of the source text:

> *"A well-regulated Militia, being necessary to the security of a free State, the right of the people to keep and bear Arms, shall not be infringed."*
> - U.S. Constitution, Amendment II;
> *Passed by Congress September 25, 1789, Ratified December 15, 1791.*

Literalists debate that only militias endorsed by a state or local government are entitled to bear arms, and not private citizens. However, the broader legally "accepted" interpretation of the language, as perpetuated by the National Rifle Association and the representatives whom this organization has installed through unrestrained campaign financing in the U.S. Congress and state houses throughout the nation, is that all individuals, including minor children and those with disabilities that impair judgement, have the Constitutionally-provided right to bear arms.

Furthermore, they posit that the "arms" referred to in the source text, is any firearm, regardless of its caliber, rate of fire, or trajectory range. And by extension, "arms" also refers to the bullets that are used within the firearms, so that bullets designed to drill into and shred human tissue or penetrate armor worn by law enforcement personnel are also protected under the language of the Constitution.

But the U.S. Constitution is not the Torah, and even the most stringent of the Rabbis and Sages who have "*paskened*" (ruled) over the centuries, have applied common sense in dealing with troubling or confusing language when human lives are at stake. We no longer communally stone to death sons accused of disobedience by their fathers, as directed in Deuteronomy to 21:18-21, or force wives suspected of infidelity to drink "bitter water" that will reveal their guilt or innocence and seal their fate, as outlined in Numbers 5:11-31. Furthermore, such high value is placed on saving a single human life, that it is permissible to break every law other than killing another human being to save one.

There is even historical precedent for changing the U.S. Constitution. It is no longer permissible to own slaves (Amendment XIII; passed by Congress January 31, 1865, ratified December 6, 1865) or to deny or abridge U.S. citizens' voting rights based on race (Amendment XV; passed by Congress January 31, 1865, ratified December 6, 1865) or gender (Amendment XIX; passed by Congress June 4, 1919, ratified August 18, 1920).

So why not change or remove the text of the Second Amendment, which was always the word of man and not the word of G-d? Obviate the need for interpretation. Just like slavery and the three-fifths clause, the Second Amendment is something that the nation's leaders at prior points in history just got wrong. Correct their mistake, so that our nation can begin to make headway toward solving a problem that leads to nearly 40,000 deaths a year – a problem that, unlike breast cancer, is actually solvable once a decision is made to "*choose life*."

How to End Gun Violence: Organize

Yael Perlman

> *Yael Perlman, daughter of Rabbi Perlman of New Light Congregation, is currently studying in Jerusalem for a gap year before college. She is interested in politics and history and has been a strong advocate for gun control for many years. This past year she led her high school in a walkout after Parkland and also went to Harrisburg with CeaseFirePA to advocate against a bill to allow teachers to have guns in schools. She is passionate about activism, running, reading, and writing.*

This Hanukkah I'm thankful that my father is alive. I am thankful that at the moment he heard that gunshot, his instincts told him to shield himself and others in a closet he didn't even know existed. This Hannukah I finally understand what miracles look like.

Not everyone was so lucky, however. Although my dad was able to survive, 11 others were murdered that day. Thousands more are killed every year because of a terrible evil in our society, guns. I know that this horrific hate crime that occurred in my synagogue one month ago was not an isolated incident and there have been many more attacks even in the month following.

2012 was the first time I ever felt the impact of gun violence. One of my sister's childhood friends, Sami Rahamim's father was killed during an attack on his store in Minnesota. Although I was only 12 at the time and very loosely connected to the incident, I felt personally impacted, not only was another Jew affected, but someone who was part of my own community. I saw Sami emerge as a gun control activist, speaking to large crowds and saying enough is enough.

That was 6 years ago, yet the same hashtag is still trending, popping up whenever a mass shooting occurs. Apparently, our message was not heard loud enough.

The day I flew back to Pittsburgh was election day in Israel, where I am studying for the year. It felt so surreal to walk around and see that on every block there were parties being held, people canvassing in the streets, and barbeques being made, all celebrating the fact that we have sovereignty in a democratic nation where we have the privilege and obligation to vote. On voting day in Israel, school and work is cancelled so that voters have full access to the polls which are open from 7AM-11PM. It felt odd to me that here I was in a country where people are excited about democracy with a 80% turnout rate on average, whereas in the US half that rate is considered high.

Americans do not feel that same sense of responsibility. Before the attack in Pittsburgh I was working with Democrats Abroad to help register people to vote in Israel. I was surprised to see that even when I handed people absentee ballots and offered to mail it for them, people still refused. One of the largest issues I see today is that Americans don't feel empowered enough to vote or are unable because of inaccessibility and voter disenfranchisement. Our responsibility is to change that mentality and show people that their voices matter and they need to speak up.

America need to learn a lesson from Israel if they wish to continue as a democratic country.

As my history teacher always says, a democracy cannot function without complete representation from the people. America was founded on the principles of no taxation without representation, yet here we are today with people denying their representation or not being able to vote because of its inaccessibility.

FairVote.org states:

> "low turnout is usually attributed to political disengagement and the belief that voting for one candidate/party or another will do little to alter public policy."

The first step to empowering people to have a political voice and showing up to the polls is making voting day a Federal holiday. We should need universal registration for all eligible voters to make voting accessible to as many people as possible.

Most people would probably agree that we don't want to be killed by guns. Although the conversation usually becomes divided at that point to the two extremes, I believe that we can work together on both political ends to create a common sense and feasible solution to the massive amounts of guns in this country.

Maybe America isn't ready yet to completely repeal all guns, but starting by making assault rifles, which have very little practical use outside of mass shootings, illegal is certainly a stepping off point. I recognize that politics, especially something as contentious as gun laws, is a slow-moving game and it often takes years to see real progress. For this reason, people often feel that they can't make a difference but that needs to change.

While I have felt so supported by the actions of those around me both in the Jewish and non-Jewish worlds, I feel that what our country truly needs right now is common sense gun laws to prevent future massacres. I hope that people feel galvanized by this attack to not only fight weeks or months after the attack, but even years if that's how long it takes to fix the problem.

When I was home I talked with a good friend, Tammy Hepps, who leads a Jewish activist group called Bend the Arc in Pittsburgh. I was expressing my grief that after Parkland so many people were moved to organize, yet nothing substantial changed. She said to me,

> "...now that they targeted the Jews, something is going to change, because the Jews know how to fucking organize."

Although it hurts me to think that this attack is what we needed to see a difference, I hope that people truly realize our desperate desire for a change in society.

This Hannukah I pray for a democracy with higher percentages of participation like in Israel and other established democracies. I hope that people continue to feel their voices heard and I pray that guns no longer rule over our lives and terrorize the places where we worship, learn, and live our everyday lives.

Remarks at a Boston Vigil in Solidarity with the Tree of Life Synagogue
Rabbi David Lerner

> *Spiritual leader of Temple Emunah, Lexington, Mass. since 2004, David Lerner also serves as the immediate past president of the Massachusetts Board of Rabbis. He is one of the founders of Community Hevra Kadisha of Greater Boston and ClergyAgainstBullets.org. After his ordination at Jewish Theological Seminary, where he was a Wexner Graduate Fellow, Rabbi Lerner served at NSS Beth El in Highland Park, IL.*

As we gather here tonight, we are still in shock. We are hurting. Even though I did not know those who were murdered, I feel as if I do. As I have read about them from friends who did know them, they were the regulars – those who show up to greet people, to create a welcoming atmosphere, to make sure there is a minyan, a quorum for the service.

Those people are found in every synagogue and church – they are the backbone of our communities.

This is also a chilling reminder that anti-Semitism still exists. We may have thought we were moving beyond it, but this week and the last few years, have, unfortunately, reminded us that this ancient hate does not seem to go away. Scratch the surface and there it is.

And it is triggered by hateful speech and rhetoric. The Mishnah some 2,000 years ago warns leaders:

> *"hakhamim, hizaharu vidivreikhem* / leaders, be careful with your words. (Avot 1:11)"

Watch what you say, be careful how you communicate. If you foment hate, it will lead certain individuals to commit acts of violence and hate.

We have just experienced two weeks of that. Hate led to an individual to send pipe bombs, to the murders of two African-Americans in Kentucky, who were killed simply because they are black, and the commission of this most heinous act in Pittsburgh.

If leaders in our country spew hate, this is the devastating result.

Holding Fast

And this unites three major issues for our community: anti-Semitism, immigration, and gun violence.

Not only is it a stark reminder of the unique hatred of anti-Semitism, but the Tree of Life synagogue was targeted because it was on a list for HIAS' [Hebrew Immigrant Aid Society] list for National Refugee Shabbat – a Shabbat when we heard from speakers about the importance of immigration, of caring for those who need refuge.

Both Temples Emunah and Isaiah participated in National Refugee Shabbat a couple of weeks ago. As Emma Lazarus wrote, "Give me your tired, your poor, your huddled masses yearning to be free…." This poem reminds us how to treat immigrants – we must not demonize them, we should treat people with kindness, all people.

And finally, the scourge of gun violence. This is an issue that continues to devastate our country unlike many other places. And this is because we do not have federal laws in place to protect us.

In our great Commonwealth we do, but nationally we do not. Since the federal assault weapons ban was not renewed, we have experienced more and more of these horrific mass shootings with AR-15 assault style weapons. Shame on all those responsible for this.

It is frightening to live in a country where such hate exists and can be acted upon. It has been happening to many groups – to different faith groups, to various ethnicities. We can draw a line from the shooting in the Charleston church to Sutherland Springs, Texas to Pittsburgh.

Something that was inconceivable a few years ago, has become more and more common.

While the climate in America has chilling echoes of an older anti-Semitism, this time it's very different.

Unlike the police in Germany before and during the Holocaust, who were ordered into civilian clothes to destroy Jewish properties, our brave police officers run into the line of fire to save Jews.

Unlike other faiths who did not stand by their Jewish sisters and brothers, today, we have received cards, letters, calls and texts from all different faith groups – Catholics, Protestants, Evangelical Christian, Unitarians, Muslims, Hindus – that they are proud to stand with us at this time means the world to us and makes this a moment to build bridges, even stronger bridges, between our communities.

Let us hold fast to our core values of civility and kindness that is part of all our faith traditions and let this terrible attack be a goad to increase our bonds as a community, creating new hope and light for us all and let us all say: Amen.

May the memories of…..

1. Joyce Fienberg, 75, of Oakland, City of Pittsburgh
2. Richard Gottfried, 65, of Ross Township
3. Rose Mallinger, 97, of Squirrel Hill
4. Jerry Rabinowitz, 66, of Edgewood Borough
5. David Rosenthal, 54, of Squirrel Hill
6. Cecil Rosenthal, 59, of Squirrel Hill (David's brother)
7. Bernice Simon, 84, of Wilkinsburg
8. Sylvan Simon, 86, of Wilkinsburg (Bernice's husband)
9. Daniel Stein, 71, of Squirrel Hill
10. Melvin Wax, 88, of Squirrel Hill
11. Irving Younger, 69, of Mt. Washington, City of Pittsburgh

…. be for a blessing.

After Pittsburgh, We Must Remember
Rabbi Menachem Creditor

> Rabbi Menachem Creditor serves as the Pearl and Ira Meyer Scholar in Residence at UJA-Federation New York. Named by Newsweek as one of the fifty most influential rabbis in America, he is the founder of Rabbis Against Gun Violence, and has served in leadership positions for American Jewish World Service, AIPAC, the Rabbinical Assembly, and the One America Movement. Among his 17 books and six albums of original Jewish music are "And Yet We Love: Poems," "Primal Prayers," and *"Olam Chesed Yibaneh/A World of Love."*

In the aftermath of the worst terrorist attack against Jewish community in US history, and days before a midterm election that stands to either endorse or turn back the tide on the erosion of human rights, the American faith community is called yet again to stand in solidarity against encroaching antisemitism and racism, two of the many faces of White Supremacy in the United States.

We must remember:

1) *We do not stand alone.* The incredible solidarity surrounding the American Jewish community defies what past generations could have imagined. This attack does not represent a nation that will stand by as Jews are hurt. This is also what it means to be a person of faith: to stand with fellow Americans of other faiths when they are targeted. We should never love others less than we are loved as we weep from our deep losses.

2) *We do not stand alone.* This attack is one of 12 Gun Violence attacks on an American house of worship in the past 3 years. The Gun Violence epidemic claims 33,000 lives every year. Yes, this attack hit the innermost heart of the Jewish community, and in the most horrifying and ironic way, this attack also proves that we are all truly American. The epidemic of weaponized American hatred includes us along with Sikhs, Muslims, African Americans, Immigrants, LGBTQ Americans, and every other minority. Which means…

3) *We dare not stand alone.* This moment of American history and this ravaging Sabbath massacre tells us that all is not well in our Republic. Hate is emboldened, and White Supremacists are somehow mainstream. This was antisemitism, yes. But it is also a diseased

American moment, where healing will only begin if we deny terrorism its goal: to isolate each of us within our particular trauma.

We are not alone, we should not make ourselves alone. Even in this incalculable pain.

The Blood of the Children Cries Out from the Ground!
Rabbi Gary S. Creditor

> *Rabbi Gary S. Creditor was tapped by Virginia Governor Tim Kaine to participate in the memorial program for the students and faculty who died as victims of Gun Violence at Virginia Tech. He has been an American Jewish leader for over 40 years, participating on countless boards and communal agencies, Jewish, interfaith, and civic. In 2003 he received his Doctorate from the Jewish Theological Seminary recognizing more than 25 years of Rabbinic service.*

Over the many years that I can remember, beginning with the assassination of President John Kennedy with a rifle, the sound of the bullet was echoed by the citation of the second amendment and the "right to bear arms." Whenever a catastrophe occurs, whoever cites past catastrophes always omits the earliest ones, which never lose their terribleness, because it is too hard, too painful, too long a list to remember to recite all the names of all the places.

I want to talk about the "Right to Live." This is not the cliché lifted from the Declaration of Independence, "life, liberty and the pursuit of happiness," even as that is a very significant statement. I want to talk about the "Right to Live" of six and seven-year olds to grow up, discover the universe, and fulfill their destinies. I want to talk about the "Right to Live" of the people dedicated to teaching them, who threw themselves in harm's way. I want to talk about the "Right to Live" of all innocent people, struggling in a difficult world, being good people, loving men and women, who are murdered, wantonly murdered by those with guns in their hands, in any place and at any time. Not just now.

I want to know something. Doesn't the "Right to Live" supersede the "right to bear arms?" Isn't there something more important than guns? Isn't there something more fundamental than the caliber of the bullet? Isn't there something more precious than the rate of fire? Doesn't the "Right to Live" trump all other rights? To paraphrase the verse from Genesis from the story of Cain and Abel, "the blood of the children, the blood of their adult defenders screams out to Me from the ground." It is to them, the dead, to our children, the living, that the answers must be given.

I want to know something. Does the "right to kill" supersede the "Right to Live?" What is the

Holding Fast

purpose of guns? I remember being a little boy with a holster and cap guns. You had to put one cap in each and it made a bang. For some reason I had a Mattel gun that used a roll of caps and you could make a lot of sustained noise. I had no idea what I was doing. I had no idea what it meant. I don't know why my parents bought them for me.

Stop the nonsense that guns don't kill! *Yes they do!* Yes, guns kill because they are held by people. Guns kill people. Guns kill animals. Killing begets killing, which begets more and more and more until there is no end! The blood of the children cries out from the ground: stop the killing! *Who needs guns?!*

I want to know something. Is the "Right to Live" held so cheaply because the profit is great from the proliferation of the "culture to kill" through video, movies, music – do you listen to the message of the lyrics? What is more important? To make money and elevate the culture of death? Or the culture of life? Is this the America we want? Is this the epitome of our society? Is this the "alabaster city?" *Is this the country that we want God to bless?*

I enjoy the old westerns on cable. Where is the blood? Where is senseless violence? None. Justice, honesty, truth were the elevated values that would triumph, but killing was not glorified. There was even a sense of remorse by the guy who was clearly good. Today it is reversed! The more gore, the more horror, the more blood and guts and cut open bodies, the more explosions and destructions. Just because there is the technical capability to show all this, do we have to? Should we? Must we? What world are we making? Do we promote fine arts? Do we esteem classical literature? Do we elevate excellent music? What do you expect to reap, when the seeds of destruction are so blatantly planted? The blood of the children cries out from the ground: make us a better world! Make us a world of peace!

I want to know something. Against whom are we bearing arms? Do we fear invasion from our neighbors to the north and south? Do we fear our neighbors who live next door? Do we intend to confront the local and state police? Would not intruders be more deterred by active alarm systems? Will the ability to defend against an intruder outweigh the number of deaths caused by people with guns who are ill-trained and ill-tempered? Will the proliferation of more guns, in a society already more armed than any in the world, make us safer, securer, surer? Are these quasi-military, high powered, quick-firing guns, the ones used to shoot duck, deer and antelope? The blood of the children cries out from the ground. They demand to know: who needs these guns?

I want to know something. I remember when living in New York it was decided to close facilities dealing with mental health, as it was deemed better to integrate these people into society at large. It never happened. If they had, they were abandoned to their families who did not have means to cope with the needs. Otherwise, they were on the streets. It really wasn't the philosophy, it was the cost. They would rather build prisons that honestly deal with the needs of society. They didn't want to deal with people. People with mental issues are "nobody's fault." They are members of our universal family. They are the easiest to cut in any budget. They are seemingly invisible. They don't have a lobby like the NRA. Now, now, it is on the agenda! The blood of the children cries out from the ground: this is the real cliff! This is the real cliff over which our world is destroyed! Fix it! Repair it! Mend it! Do not ignore us!

I want to know something. How many innocent deaths will it take for our elected officials to be leaders with moral backbones and not wimps who pander for votes? Where is their moral courage to face the mirror and know that day after day they have labored in society's vineyard to make each hamlet, each town, each county, each city better for each boy and girl, infant and adult, young and old, reach and poor, healthy and ill? How many tears must be shed by human beings? How much blood must spill in movie theatres, college campuses, high schools, elementary schools, shopping mall parking lots? How many hearts must break when the bell tolls as each name is read, as each tender body is buried? What must it take for delegates, senators, representatives, and president will finally act?

Until then, every morning, noon and night, at the break of dawn and the setting of the sun, in the dead of night and the brightness of the midday sun.

The blood of the children cries out from the ground! And it will continue to cry and cry, scream upon scream, until someone, someone will give them an answer.

Looking Evil in the Eye
Rabbi Joshua Hammerman

> *Rabbi Joshua Hammerman is spiritual leader of Temple Beth-El in Stamford, Conn. He wrote this originally for the New York Jewish Week. The essay will also be included in his upcoming book, "Mensch Marks: Life Lessons of a Human Rabbi – Wisdom for Untethered Times," to be published in April by HCI Books.*

The attack on Jewish worshipers in Pittsburgh hit me very personally. My mother's funeral was the same weekend, so for me and my community, it was truly a tale of two *shivas*. I sat publicly for ten hours each day, because I believe in the importance of that ritual and in its healing power, and those endless hours enabled me to have real conversations with about 400 people. While people came to comfort me, they also looked to me for comfort, and our collective Jewish people's *shiva* and my personal *shiva* fused together as one. We sat together and mourned the untimely deaths of innocent, vulnerable people, people at prayer, people who had only love in their hearts. I felt helpless to do anything about it – and yet, in my community, the healing took place, down in the trenches of the mourning bench, one on one on one on one.

Among the questions that continually arose that week is one that may not seem very significant when compared to the stinging loss of 11 innocent lives, but is vexing nonetheless: Should Jews turn the other cheek?

A few days after the attack, the Rev. Eric S.C. Manning, leader of the Emanuel African Methodist Episcopal Church in Charleston, S.C., where nine parishioners were murdered in 2015, paid a *shiva* call to Pittsburgh, where he embraced Rabbi Jeffrey Myers of the Tree of Life congregation. Their shared grief moved us all, but at the same time it brought attention to one aspect of the two cases that wasn't shared.

Following the Charleston attack, the victims' families famously forgave the murderer as he stood before them in court. By contrast, as The New York Times reported, the Jews of Pittsburgh had no intentions of being so forgiving. The Times article states that Jews interviewed said they had been too busy burying the dead and trekking from *shiva* to *shiva* to devote much thought to the killer. It then adds,

> "But Jewish theologians also explained that *their tradition, rooted more in the retributive justice of the Old Testament than the turn-the-cheek ethos*

> *of the New Testament, takes a different approach to forgiveness."*

Yes, it's true, Judaism does take a different approach. The article goes on to explain, correctly, that the Jewish concept of *teshuvah* calls on the perpetrator to seek forgiveness from the victim before having any hope of absolution. Then it adds that Pittsburgh mourners "felt little instinct to forgive the person responsible for such horror."

Clearly, there is a difference in how the victims of Pittsburgh and Charleston approached similar calamities. But whenever someone traces things back to the "retributive justice of the Old Testament God," an enormous red flag is raised. There are many images of God depicted in the Hebrew Bible, some more vengeful and others more loving. The thunderous God of the Exodus Sinai narrative is later encountered by Elijah, in the very same place, as a *"still, small voice."* And that kinder-gentler New Testament God seemed to conveniently forget to turn-the-cheek during the Crusades and Inquisition.

The notion of a perpetually vengeful Old Testament God has inspired stereotypic images of hard-hearted Jews, even though the Torah explicitly prohibits taking revenge and holding grudges.

Why does Judaism not encourage the unconditional embrace of your enemy? When you turn your cheek, you are no longer looking at your offender in the eye, face to face. True reconciliation can only occur when two human beings can truly see what is human in the other, and how each of us is created in the Divine image. But there are times when such authentic encounters simply can't happen.

The Pittsburgh perpetrator showed no signs of remorse during his appearance in court, and it is doubtful that he will when he stands trial. It would be a grave injustice to blindly forgive him.

After the Charleston massacre, I attended a prayer vigil, at which I heard a presentation by Inni Kaur, a representative of the Stamford Sikh community, reflecting on her own faith group's experiences.

It should be noted that the Sikh community suffered a similar massacre, at a temple in Oak Creek, Wis., in 2012. Unfortunately, no religious group is immune to such attacks. The image of people at prayer or study seeing their sanctuary violated, having the pastoral serenity and love of neighbor rendered instantaneously into a garish nightmare, is one that cuts across cultures.

Holding Fast

My Sikh friend recalled Oak Creek, and how the community rallied together and preached love over hate, and, like Charleston, even forgave the perpetrator. She said, "These communities have shown us that faith helps endure any hardship, even the most unspeakable suffering. Faith does not mean we forget pain or grief. Faith means that we live free of hate. These monumental acts of forgiveness compel each and every one of us to work towards ending the racial terror that exists in our country today; to find ways to look beyond the boundaries of race, color, ethnicity and see the Oneness in all."

So "forgiving" enemies are not about letting them off the hook — it's about looking them in the eye and telling them, loud and clear, that they have not succeeded in driving a wedge between groups. It's about achieving a greater societal goal by suppressing base urges. In Charleston, Oak Creek, Orlando and now Pittsburgh, the ideology of hate was drowned in a sea of love.

In Charleston, the victims' supreme gesture of love yielded tangible results — the removal of the Confederate flag from the state capitol. One hate-driven young man accomplished in one evening what Martin Luther King could not accomplish in a lifetime, at least with regard to the shunning of this symbol of hate.
One might say that for the bereaved of Charleston, forgiveness was the best revenge.

Jews Respond to American Gun Violence

For the Jews of Pittsburgh, the best revenge against the particular hatred espoused by white nationalists has not been to turn the other cheek, but to build stronger bridges to other targeted communities, like African Americans and Muslims, who have shown such love in the wake of the attack.

And that love was reflected at the ballot box, where polls suggest that late deciders in the 2018 midterm elections swung away from harsh nativism, following pipe bomb attacks on Democratic leaders and the Pittsburgh pogrom.

(Yes, these days pogroms no longer require angry mobs with pitchforks; now all it takes is a single crazy hater with an AR-15).

Also quite noticeable was the lack of support for NRA endorsed candidates, particularly in the suburbs, and the newfound electoral confidence of those who support common sense gun laws. A generation of NRA dominance of American politics may be nearing its end.

As voters decided "enough is enough," our newest Jewish martyrs changed America, while their bereaved turned not the other cheek, but perhaps the tide of history.

Anti-Semitism and Anti-Black Racism Both Advance White Supremacy[5]

Jeanné Isler and Timi Gerson

> Jeanné Isler and Timi Gerson are Vice Presidents of Engagement and Content respectively at the National Committee for Responsive Philanthropy (www.ncrp.org).

This fall, our communities came under physical attack again.

In one week in October, a shooter screaming *"all Jews must die"* killed 11 elderly Jewish congregants at a synagogue in Pittsburgh. Two Black senior citizens, Maurice Stallard and Vickie Jones, were murdered in cold blood in a grocery store in Kentucky. The Trump administration sent more than 5,000 troops to the U.S.-Mexico border to inflict state-sponsored

---

[5] Original version published on November 15, 2018 on the blog of the National Committee for Responsive Philanthropy at
https://www.ncrp.org/2018/11/anti-semitism-and-anti-black-racism-both-advance-white-supremacy.html

violence against a caravan of Central American refugees seeking political asylum.

The men who perpetrated this violence are very clear on the connection between these acts. The question progressives need to ask ourselves is: *Are we?*

White supremacists have a twisted worldview in which "anti-Semitism forms the theoretical core of white nationalism," according to research deftly laid out by Eric Ward of Oregon-based anti-hate advocacy group Western States Center.[6] Racism, xenophobia and anti-Semitism are not separate strands of hatred for these ethno-nationalists, but rather deeply intertwined and mutually reinforcing.
So too must be our strategies for combating it.
Some in our communities have always understood that our safety lies in solidarity. Ancient rabbis taught:

> "We sustain the non-Jewish poor with the Jewish poor, visit the non-Jewish sick with the Jewish sick, and bury the non-Jewish dead with the Jewish dead, for the sake of peace."[7]

---

[6] Ward, Eric K. "Skin in the Game: How Anti-Semitism Animates White Nationalism" The Public Eye magazine, Summer 2017 edition.
[7] Babylonian Talmud (Gittin 61a)

Thousands of years later, Black civil rights leader Fannie Lou Hamer put it more succinctly: "Nobody's free until everybody's free."

Our practice, however, too often fails to act on this communal knowledge.

In the 20 years that both of us –a white Jewish woman and a Black Christian woman - have been active in social justice organizing, it has been vanishingly rare to find a mention of anti-Semitism, much less a discussion of the intersection of it with anti-Black racism and xenophobia, in progressive spaces.

Anti-Semitism does not fit neatly into American narratives around oppression. And very little has been done by most people who would otherwise consider themselves social justice-minded activists or funders to understand it. Part of the complexity is the small gain towards attaining whiteness[8]" that the majority of the U.S. Jewish community has been able to make in the last few decades. This (conditional) whiteness is used explicitly and repeatedly to divide our communities from each other.

In the wake of the Pittsburgh tragedy, the fact that state-sponsored protection in the form of extra police was extended to Jewish synagogues

---

[8] For an exploration of this subject, please see: Brodkin, Karen. *How Jews Became White Folks and What That Says About Race in America*. New Brunswick, N.J: Rutgers University Press, 1998

and schools contrasts markedly with the official response to similar attacks on Black churches.

Regardless of whether you believe police protection is useful or desirable, it bears noting that Black churches were not offered it despite the historic and present trend of white supremacist violence where African-Americans gather to worship. This kind of disparity perpetuates nominal divides between two communities that are facing threats connected at the root.

Another way we are divided is through "scandals" that seek to obfuscate the difference between the real violent threat of white supremacists vs. the ignorance of anti-Semitic and anti-Black comments that occasionally rear their ugly head among our communities. We do not believe that the echo chamber created to fan the flames of such scandals into mutual mistrust or worse is an accidental occurrence. Rather, it is a divisive tactic expressly designed to strengthen white supremacy by distracting us from our shared values and goals, and obscuring the clear and present danger represented by the white nationalist movement.

To create the world we want, we cannot let white nationalists define our relationship with each other. We must deepen our analysis and education about the connection between anti-

Semitism and anti-Black racism in our country[9]. We must dialogue with each other.

Instead of excluding groups who are mostly values aligned, but may be ignorant about this connection, it is our task to make space to wrestle with hard history towards joint action.

It is our hope that with these terrible massacres, we are motivated to search the blind spots that leave us vulnerable to division and violence and instead expose them to the light. Our very lives depend on it.

---

[9] Two great resources are the Jews for Racial and Economic Justice (JFREJ) toolkit "Understanding Anti-Semitism" available online at https://jfrej.org/wp-content/uploads/2017/11/JFREJ-Understanding-Antisemitism-November-2017-1.pdf.

Sermon for Solidarity Shabbat after the Pittsburgh Tragedy
(Parashat Chaye Sarah)
Rabbi Joseph R. Black

> Rabbi Black has been the Senior Rabbi of Temple Emanuel since 2010, previously serving as rabbi of Congregation Albert in Albuquerque, New Mexico from 1996-2010. His books and music have been featured by the PJ library and he was honored by Moment magazine as one of the top ten male performers in American Jewish music as well as one of the top ten children's performers in American Jewish music.

Where were you last Saturday?

How did you hear about the tragic events that took place in Pittsburgh?

I was sitting in our Chapel, celebrating the Bat Mitzvah of a wonderful young girl when my Apple Watch started to buzz frantically with texts from colleagues, family members and concerned congregants. I normally do not respond to text messages in the middle of a service – unless I am texting our Executive Director Steve Stark to tell him that it's too hot or too cold in the chapel.... This time I stepped out and looked at the news.

When I saw that there was a mass shooting at a Synagogue, my blood ran cold. While the final tally of destruction had not yet been posted at that time, it was clear that what was taking place was going to be horrific and life-changing for the American Jewish community. During the service, I briefly shared what news I had learned to those present. When we took out the Shoah Scroll and told the story of its journey from Kolin, to a warehouse in Prague, to the Westminster Synagogue in London, England, and eventually here to Temple Emanuel – where it was placed in the very ark that where it began – and ended up as the spiritual center or our congregation – the raw emotions that I was experiencing were shared by everyone in our chapel.

And so now we sit – one week later – after so many things have transpired: here in our community and around the country. In a little more than 24 hours after news of the shooting reached us, our community rallied and together with the ADL, Jewish Colorado and the Rocky Mountain Rabbinical Council, we put together a Solidarity Vigil in which over 3,000 souls came together in this sanctuary – and overflowing into our foyer and Social Hall. To see representatives from the Christian, Muslim and Sikh communities joining together on our Bema - along with the leadership of our city and State and Federal government and law enforcement was overwhelming. The tears that flowed, the powerful words that were shared, the anger angst and love combined with grief that filled our sacred space provided a necessary space and time to process and express our feelings. In the days following the Vigil, we have received hundreds of calls, letters, flowers, emails and visits from well-wishers from multiple communities who wanted to show their love and support to the Jewish people. Truly, this is a time of both horror and wonder as we have witnessed both the worst and the best of humanity coming together at one and the same time.

Even though the last of the funerals for the victims of this shooting was today, Jews around the world have been mourning since we received word of this horror. In Jewish tradition, after 7 days of mourning, we symbolically rise from our mourning and conclude Shiva. This Shabbat, we join with synagogues around the world as we come together in our grief and solidarity to remember our dead, recite the mourner's kaddish and look ahead to the future.

As I thought about what I might say tonight at this service, I looked into this week's Torah portion, Chaye Sarah.

Like many portions in the book of Genesis, Chaye Sarah has multiple stories that are woven into the narrative. It begins with the death of Sarah and ends with the death of Abraham. Abraham purchases the cave of Machpelah in Hebron. He then sends his servant to Canaan to find a wife for Isaac. At the end of the parasha, Abraham dies.

Our text reads as follows:

> "Then Abraham passed on, and died in a good old age, an old man, and full of years; and was gathered to his people. And his sons Isaac and Ishmael buried him in the cave of Machpelah, in the field of Ephron the son of Zohar the Hittite, which is before Mamre; The field which Abraham purchased from the Hittites; there was Abraham buried, and Sarah his wife." (Genesis 25:8-10)

One of the most remarkable aspects of this text is the fact that Isaac and Ishmael bury their father together. If you recall, the last we have heard of Ishmael was when Abraham sent him and his mother, Hagar, out into the wilderness because Sarah did not want Ishmael to be a threat to Isaac and his eventual birthright. Abraham had scarred Ishmael by casting him away. He also had scarred Isaac by almost slaughtering him on Mt. Moriah.

Abraham's death unites these two brothers. They both understand pain. They both understand loss. They both realize that, no matter what events have taken place in their lives, they are bound together by a common task and purpose.

Isaac and Ishmael had cause to hate their father –and to hate each other. The Midrash, in particular is filled with stories of their warfare. Yet, at the end of our parasha they come together in peace in order to bury Abraham. They realize that, despite their history, they are linked together. In burying Abraham, they are also symbolically burying the past and moving ahead to the future.

If there is anything that we can learn from this horrible tragedy, it may be found in the outpouring of love and solidarity that we experienced on Sunday. I truly believe that is a reflection of the best that our nation has to offer. So much of the language we are hearing is divisive; the politics of isolationism and victimization have taken a toll on our souls. Especially in the days leading up to November 6 – election day- everyone is on edge. To see people from multiple communities coming together to show their love and support in the shadow of terror is both an affirmation of what we, as a nation are all about and a powerful reflection of how we, like Isaac and Ishmael, can rise up above our divisions in solidarity and celebrate the awareness that we are all created in the image of God.

Tonight is November 2th. In one week, November 9th, 2018, we will be commemorating the 80th Anniversary of Kristallnacht – the night of the Broken Glass. Kristallnacht was the beginning of the end of European Jewry.

On that night, 80 years ago, Nazi thugs burned synagogues and destroyed Jewish businesses throughout Germany and Austria. Jews were beaten publicly in the streets. Men were rounded up and sent to concentration camps. Hitler and his thugs waited to see what the reaction would be from world leaders. The deafening silence that ensued in the shadow of terror was a clear sign to the Nazis that they had a green light to take whatever steps they wanted to rid the world of the "Jewish problem."

My mother and her parents lived through Krystallnacht. They were among the lucky ones. One month later they were able to get a visa out of Germany and immigrate to the United States.

The memory of that night of terror is indelibly linked into the consciousness of our people. From the pain and horror of November 9th and the darkness and evil that it spawned, we have emerged - wounded, yet determined to honor the memory of those who perished in the Shoah and rebuild our lives, our people and our homeland.

Holding Fast

Like Isaac and Ishmael – we were and are united by our grief and our loss.

If we can survive and thrive in the aftermath of that historical and spiritual darkness, how much the more so are we obligated to persevere in the shadow of the Tree of Life Synagogue massacre?

Let us have no illusions. The battle against evil is not over. The haters who have become emboldened in recent months will not disappear overnight. They will lie beneath the surface as they always have – waiting for the next opportunity to strike. We must remain vigilant and defiant. We know that though there are those who seek to use violence fear and intimidation to accomplish their ends – we, as a people and nation must never allow hatred to determine the path along which we walk together.

Now is a time to come together and find unity in our historical memory and the vision of a world that , while incomplete, awaits for each of us to use our talents, strengths and faith to perfect God's Creation.

We owe it to ourselves.

We owe it to the memory of those who are no longer with us

We owe it to our nation to move on from our divisions and focus on ways that we can work to perform the mitzvah of Tikkun Olam – of repairing our all too imperfect world.

Zichronam Livracha – may the memory of the righteous be for an eternal blessing.

AMEN

A Prophetic Response to Gun Violence[10]
Rabbi Menachem Creditor

> *Rabbi Menachem Creditor is the Pearl and Ira Meyer Scholar in Residence of UJA-Federation New York and the founder of Rabbis Against Gun Violence.*

In this moment, what does God want of us?

What are we called to do in the face of great devastation, some of which receives our nation's attention, most of which doesn't? How can we, in our efforts to extend God's Healing to our sisters and brothers, address Gun Violence, a terrible tear in the fabric of our nation?

What is a Prophet? How does she hear the Divine Weeping and call all God's children to awareness and action?

---

[10] This reflection was first presented on January 29, 2013 at the White House as part of a national clergy gathering in response to the Sandy Hook Massacre in Newtown, CT.

Hear the call of Isaiah, who reminded us that God wants, more than anything else, for us to

> ...unlock the fetters of wickedness, untie the cords of the yoke, to let the oppressed go free, to break off every yoke. ...to share your bread with the hungry, and to take the wretched poor into our homes; When you see the naked, clothe him, and do not ignore your own brother.[11]

The great Rabbi Abraham Joshua Heschel lived this lesson well. He reminded us that human beings, living Images of God, must have prophetic faith. But the faith of a prophet, Heschel taught,

> ...does not mean... to dwell in the shadows of old ideas... [or] to live off an inherited estate of doctrines and dogmas. In the realm of the spirit, only [one] who is a pioneer is able to be an heir.[12]

The prophets are the ones who demanded justice in the world, starting with Abraham's challenge to God "Shall not the judge of all the earth do justice?"[13]

We must feel fiercely[14] like the Prophets of old. And, like the prophets, as today's prophetic witnesses, we must see no divide between the political and the spiritual, for a world without

---

[11] Isaiah 58:6-7
[12] Heschel, *Man is Not Alone*, p. 164
[13] Genesis 18:25
[14] Heschel, *The Prophets*, p. 5

Holding Fast

fierce feeling is a world without spirit, and a religious tradition with nothing to say to the world is no longer engaged in bringing God's world to a more blessed day.

It is possible to lose hope. This world gives little encouragement to hope. And that is why we do what we do, why we answer our call with all the ferocity we can muster. We will not "stand idly by while the blood of our neighbors"[15] continues to be spilled.

Say it with me a tragic litany: *Newtown. Aurora. Columbine. Tucson. Virginia Tech. [Charleston, Parkland, Las Vegas, Pittsburgh, colleges, high schools, grade schools, baseball games, hospitals, movie theaters, naval bases, homes, streets…]*

But now acknowledge with me also: These massacres received national attention. But the three high school students shot this past Thursday in Albany, CA did not. Nor did the seven people killed and six wounded in gun violence this past Saturday in Chicago, including a 34-year-old man whose mother had already lost three other children to shootings.

A prophet does not feel for SOME of these. A Prophet feels every death as her own. A Prophet writhes with God's Pain, their soul contorting in ways that make it hard to breathe.

---

[15] Leviticus 19:15

I repeat: It is possible to lose hope. But we are not allowed. Hope is our call. Extending hope, enabling peace, offering prophetic witness to the awful events of our day and communicating, over and over and over and over and over that God's world deserves better than fear and greed. God's world depends upon the work our hands, to be friends and partners together, to engage with our elected officials and law enforcement and teachers and others, to notice the violence that doesn't get reported, to breathe in and breathe out and breathe in and breathe out. Because if we don't, less of God's Work gets done.

I say that there are those in our country to whom Jeremiah would say today:

> On your shirt is found the life-blood of guiltless poor. Yet in spite of all these things, you say 'I am innocent.'[16]

If we are to avoid complicity in the growing violence of our country, we must remain every vigilant as witness to "the callousness of man" and not allow our heart to do what it wishes, which would be to "obliterate the memories, to calm the nerves, and to silence our conscience."[17]

---

[16] Jeremiah 2:14
[17] Heschel, *The Reasons for My Involvement in the Peace Movement*

The Prophets call us:

Do Not Be Calm.
Do Not Forget.
Do Not Be Silent.

Friends, given the pressure on us, on everyone, I invite you right now to take a deep breath. Allow your body to experience a little more air. Breathe it in. Remember your power, God's Spirit, of which we are each but fragments.

There is great fear on the part of some that any response to Gun Violence is a rejection of the Second Amendment of our Constitution. *Fear.* There are those whose very work is the proliferation of weapons of war on the streets of our cities and across our great nation with one over-riding concern: profit. *Greed.*

And this heady cocktail of Fear and Greed makes our work as religious leaders difficult. But we know that sacred work is not easy work. We do not answer to Fear and Greed. And we are not going to respond with hate to fear and greed – that is the way to make the fear and greed ever-stronger. We're going to outlast them.

There are those who have said that any response to Gun Violence reduces the U.S. Constitution into a blank slate for anyone's graffiti. *Lies.* It is our shared belief in the possibility of this country, our commitment to a democracy of free women and men of every orientation and color in the rainbow that gives us the courage to bend the historical arc of this country once again toward justice.

We, faith leaders who call God with an infinite variety of Holy Names, are called in this moment to do sacred work and to weather the intense fear and greed in a moment of national fragility. We will face the deaths our country continues to endure at the hands of unfettered Gun Violence, at the hands of those who follow profit margins and ignore those marginalized by society.

Heschel taught us, in the name of the Prophets, that "the heart of human dignity is the ability to be responsible."[18]

We call upon each other and all who will listen to be strong and resolute. We will "walk humbly with God"[19] and we will refuse to ignore the suffering of God's children.

For while, as Heschel said, in a moral world, "some may be guilty, but all are responsible."[20]

---

[18] Heschel, *Required: A Moral Ombudsman*, United Synagogue Review, Fall 1971
[19] Micah 6:8
[20] Heschel, *The Prophets*, xix

Holding Fast

And so we pray together, women and men of faith, recognizing that which we have in common

May our great nation be safe place, where "every person may lie down with no one terrifying them."[21]

May people of every faith – *and of no faith* – work together to make the necessary changes to heal our nation from the scourge of Gun Violence.

My fellow clergy, women and men who serve God by serving all People, may the passion of the Prophets infuse our work, our words, our deeds, our thoughts – *every fiber of our souls* - so that when we do speak, we can cry more freely with God's Holy Tears and feel strengthened through that fierce feeling.

May the Source of Life whose Spirit awaits realization in every human breath fill us with hope and sustained determination us as we seek an end to all this death in our land.

Amen.

---

[21] Leviticus 26:6, paraphrased

Jews Respond to American Gun Violence

Targets
Lisa Rappaport

> *Lisa Rappaport is an educator and Rabbinic student in the Aleph Ordination Program. She is also a Rabbinic Intern at Congregation Netivot Shalom in Berkeley, CA. Lisa is the author of Divrei Nichum: Comforting Words During Times of Loss, A collection of poems for mourners. She lives in the East Bay with her hilarious husband and two dynamic daughters, aged 11 and 16.*

A week after the
Tree of Life Synagogue was terrorized
and our people were traumatized…

A stranger in a convenience store
asks if we were Jewish.

I freeze.
All four of us silent.
Why the question?
Why am I afraid?
What makes us obvious?
My husband's kippah?

Finally an answer.
Yes. We are Jewish...

My daughter tells me later,
"It was weird when that
guy asked if we were Jewish...
I wondered if he wanted to kill us."

Targets.

Shrivelling. Cowering. Hysterical inside.

In 2018, in the United States,
this thought burrows,
worming through her brain
and registers as a
legitimate possibility.
How can this be?

***

Gunfire erupts in
Sandy Hook Elementary.
I have my own first grader.
Heart pounds.
Too close to home.

Teenagers full of promise,
and the staff who faithfully support them,
are murdered in Parkland, Florida.
My older daughter is a freshman in high school.
Throat tightens.
It *could* have been her.

But then 49 people are murdered
at Pulse in Orlando.
My 13 year old
just told us she was gay.

Targets.

Body stiffens.
Part of me dies.
My daughter is a *target*.
Not because of where she *happened*
to be on a particular day
but because of *who* she *is* every moment.

On a Shabbat morning,
eleven members
of our Jewish community
are shot to death,
in the refuge of Synagogue,
while chanting ancient *prayers*,
on the holiest day of the week.

Targets.

Implosion.
Full suffocation of soul,
descending, drifting down, down
into a dark chasm of endless wails.
And simultaneously something
rises and rages and burns inside.
This is my home.
This is us.

My *PEOPLE* are targets.

***

Again,
hatred of difference is the driver.
Intolerance pulls the trigger.

I won't always
have a first grader
or a high schooler.
But my daughter is gay,
and we are Jewish.

When the need
to annihilate is calculated,
when it has a clear focus,
when hate of other drives the urge to
erase a people,
eliminate a way of life,
destroy a culture,
extinguish the possibility of choice...

...this is a different kind of violence,
a different kind of terror.

The next time a gunman
rains bullets and horror,
anyone of us might be lucky enough
to *randomly* avoid a location.

Not my day to be at
the movie theater

or the mall,
or a fast food joint,
or a concert.

I'm not in
first grade
or high school
or college.

We *might* be able to avoid *these* storms.

But when it's about who we are?
Oh my God!
When it's about *WHO* WE ARE...!

Randomness turns specific.
The bullet aims squarely at me.

Targets.

For some of us,
there are things
we cannot randomly
or conveniently avoid.

We are gay.
We are Jewish.
Our name is Rappaport.

A Prayer for One Who Enters a Synagogue
Rabbi Jill Zimmerman

> *Rabbi Jill Zimmerman is a rabbi-at-large who teaches core spiritual principles and practices in ways that enrich people's daily lives. She leads Hineni, an online Jewish community, teaches widely as a Scholar-in-Residence, and meets with people looking for spiritual guidance and support via video or in-person. She was ordained at Hebrew Union College, and has been trained in Jewish meditation and mindfulness.*

Pause as you stand before the entrance, and say a brief prayer: *"May I and my fellow worshippers be protected."*

Touch the mezuzah,
bring your fingers to your lips in a kiss,
remember why you are here.

Notice your intention:
to listen, to learn, to seek light.

Greet the greeters and deeply thank them for their kindness in welcoming all the souls that will enter into this sacred space, because what was once a mitzvah now has some danger attached: *First Defenders from Those Who Would Do Us Harm.*

Gather your prayer book,
your tallit,
your Chumash.

Sit next to a friendly face.
You are now partners
in whatever experience will ensue,
merely by being in the same circle of energy.

Say a silent blessing
for the joy of human contact,
and a prayer for safety and peace this day.

As the music swarms and the prayers build one on top of the other,
The circle grows tighter and
you become aware that
you are on a journey together
through the past and future and the now.

You ride the ebb & flow,
and you take flight together…
You remember the dead,
you speak of oneness,
you remember all the ways you are grateful.

Holding Fast

Your final words are ones of peace: *Oseh Shalom*.
May the One who makes peace…

You realize what a holy journey this is, to pray,
learn and sing together.

Before Pittsburgh,
and before Charlottesville,
You may have taken all this for granted.
But No More.

Hatred has come once again to our People.
And yes, precautions need to be taken.
Maybe armed guards at the door.

It dawns on you that gathering as Jews in America is now an act of bravery.

You don't know if there will be swastikas painted on the synagogue walls or tiki torches burning around the corner.
But you still go.

You breathe in your own courage,
you bless your own self for your strength.
You keep on showing up,
as generations did before.

Bless your heart,
bless those who greet you,
those who protect you,
bless those who come and remove the anti-Semitic graffiti off your walls,

bless those who come and sit next to you.
Bless the rabbi and cantor who come to lead & inspire.

Bless the custodians who clean.

FILL THIS HOLY PLACE WITH BLESSINGS and PRESENCE.

"It is a Tree of Life to all who hold fast to it."

Amen.

Prayer after Tragedy: *Hashkiveinu*
Rabbi David Paskin

> *Rabbi David Paskin is an accomplished spiritual leader, singer/songwriter, entertainer, Jewish futurist, social activist, award-winning Jewish educator and founding rabbi of OHEL. In 2018, David was honored to be chosen as a Rabbinic Peacemaker Fellow by the One America Movement. Prior to moving to Florida, David served as the rabbi and spiritual leader of Temple Beth Abraham in Canton, Massachusetts for seventeen years. David currently serves as the Director of Youth and Family Engagement at Temple Sinai of North Dade and the Educational Director of the Institute of Jewish Knowledge and Learning.*

Dear God,

As we settle into your sukkah of peace on this Shabbat help us open our lips to declare Your praise - and our rage. Help us find the words to denounce hatred and bigotry. Help our lips celebrate Your Presence in every human being. Help our words create and heal worlds rather than destroy them.

And God, when we are done resting, when we are done sharing words and prayers, when we have been refreshed by Your sukkat shalom, your shelter of peace - help us to stop talking and start working. Give us the strength and the courage to pray with our legs and our arms. Teach us that if we rely on prayers alone we would still be standing at the shores of the Reed Sea waiting for You to save us.

Help us find the courage to be like Nachshon ben Aminadav - to dive into the waters and use them to quench the fires of violence, ugliness, racism, xenophobia, homophobia, anti-Semitism and hatred. Let our prayers and our words be a starting point. Let this Shabbat be a beginning. Let Your tent of peace on this Shabbat remind us that we must build our own tents of peace. You created our world and gave it to us to work and to tend. Help us not forget that we are Your partners in Creation.

Olam Chesed Yibaneh - We must build this world from love.

Where God Is
Stacey Zisook Robinson

> Stacey Zisook Robinson is a poet and essayist who lives in Chicago. She works as a Poet/Scholar-in-Residence, creating workshops to explore the connection between poetry, prayer and text. She blogs at staceyzrobinson.blogspot.com, and is a regular contributor to kveller.com, the Reform Judaism blog and Ritual Well. Her book, Dancing in the Palm of God's Hand, was published in 2015, and her newest, a book of poetry, A Remembrance of Blue, was released in November 2017.

There is no place that God is not;
even in the barrel of a gun.
Bullets sing their own psalm,
a deadly hymn to the True Judge,
the Creator of us all.

There is no place that God is not.

Perhaps that is why God asks us -
pleads for us -
to sing a new song
for all the earth to hear,
to drown out the ugly and

sibilant crackle of bullets,
whose only benediction is
one of destruction and pain.

There is no place that God is not.

The Courage to Press Forward
Rabbi Shawn Israel Zevit

> *An accomplished singer and guitarist, Rabbi Shawn Zevit is a founding member of the popular Jewish musical group, Shabbat Unplugged. He has led Shabbaton programs, been Guest-Artist and Scholar-in-Residence in more than 100 congregations and havurot. Among his many publications is his most recent book Brotherkeepers: New Explorations in Jewish Masculinity and Offerings of the Heart: Money and Values in Faith Community.*

Praying for the souls of the dead,
the support for the survivors and their families
and the courage to press forward
with gun control in this country.
Radical love is the antidote for radical hate.
The heart of our work is recognizing
that our humanity unites all of us.
We must use every ounce of our being
to counter this culture
of dehumanization that infects our
communities.

We lift up prayers for victims,
families and friends.
We sit in protest or rise
 and walk in activist spirit
In the pursuit of Tzedek (Justice)
and Rachamim (Loving Compassion)
God is in this Place
And we must know it!

Jews Respond to American Gun Violence

A Tree of Life
Rabbi Ben Herman

Dedicated in honor of the birth of Leora Rose Herman on December 6, 2018

> *Rabbi Ben Herman was ordained from JTS in 2011 and is currently the rabbi of the Jericho Jewish Center on Long Island. The focus of his rabbinate is Every Person Counts, and he works tirelessly to integrate his passion for "living Judaism" into the communities he serves. Ben is married to Karina and they have two beautiful daughters: Ariela Shira and Leora Rose.*

As I look in my newborn daughter's eyes
I recognize the preciousness of her life.
She did not arrive when we planned
That only intensified the light she brought us.

We are a people who value life
Life is always stronger than death.
Life is not an accident to be squandered
Rather it is G-d's most precious gift.

Those who take the lives of others
Will not see their designs bear fruit.
Our Torah is a Tree of Life
Bringing vitality to all who hold fast to it.

As I look into my newborn daughter's eyes
I see the gift of new life
She has already brought
so much light and vitality

A Hanukkah blessing for our entire family.

I know that while her body is fragile
She has an inner strength.
We are fragile after Pittsburgh
Yet we have an inner strength.

Our love for Judaism only deepens
After someone tries to scare us.
My love for my daughter only increased
After being scared by her early birth.

Let us always remember
Love is stronger than hate.
Those who seek to destroy who we are
Will only make us stronger.

Afterword:
Why Pittsburgh Matters
Rabbi Jeffrey Salkin

Rabbi Jeffrey K. Salkin is the spiritual leader of Temple Solel in Hollywood, FL, and a noted writer and social commentator. This essay is excerpted from his blog, Martini Judaism: for those who want to be shaken and stirred, published by Religion News Service.

We are shocked, but we are not surprised.

How could we be surprised? The novelist Rebecca West once said that Jews, having suffered so much, have an "unsurprisable mind." Did we think that we, the American Jewish community, could splash blood upon our communal door and thus ward off the twin angels of hatred and death?

When we witnessed the madness in Charlottesville — "The Jews will not replace us!" — could we not have imagined that this could happen?

Anti-Semitism is the oldest hatred in history. It might also be the oldest "ism" in history, the oldest living ideology. It is the only cultural thread that binds our civilization to that of the ancient Egyptians, and the ancient Persians, and the ancient Greeks, and the ancient Romans, and the early Christians, and to medieval Christians, and to Islam, and to modern scientific racist theories. It is the one thing that all of those cultures have in common.

As Gavin Langmuir, in his book "History, Religion, and Antisemitism," writes:

> *"anti-Semitism is the hostility aroused by the irrational thinking about 'Jews.'"*

We are shocked — but, if we are surprised, it is because we American Jews have had so little actual experience of lethal anti-Semitism — despite the increase in anti-Semitic acts.

Consider the American Jews who have died — simply because they were Jews.

> • Leo Frank, the factory manager in Atlanta, who was falsely accused and lynched for the murder of a young factory girl, in 1915.
> • Alan Berg, the Denver talk radio host, killed in 1984 by members of the white nationalist group The Order.
> • Yankel Rosenbaum, killed during the Crown Heights riots in 19
> • Ari Halberstam, 16, riding in a van of Chabad students, shot to death in 1994 on a ramp, which has been renamed in his memory, leading to the Brooklyn Bridge.
> • Pamela Waechter, director of the Seattle Federation annual fundraising campaign, who was shot to death in the Seattle Federation offices in 2006.

Holding Fast

Yes, there were also non-Jews who died in attacks aimed at Jews, Jewish institutions or places that evoke Jewish memory.

According to my estimate, the total number of Jews killed, before the shooting in Pittsburgh: five.

Which means — that the death toll in Pittsburgh immediately tripled the number of American victims of lethal anti-Semitism. Yesterday was the worst day in American Jewish history.

The attack on Tree of Life Synagogue in Pittsburgh was not only an attack on Jews. It was not only an attack on Judaism. It was an attack on all that we hold sacred.

First, sacred places. The entire Pittsburgh neighborhood of Squirrel Hill is a sacred place. Fred Rogers located his Neighborhood of Make Believe in Squirrel Hill, because it is a magical place. It is unique: perhaps the last Jewish shtetl in the United States, a small town in which generations of Jews and Jewish institutions flourish; a neighborhood of such beauty, diversity and dignity that, typically, when Jews became wealthier they did not leave — they simply moved to a different house.

In the words of the TV sitcom "Cheers": "Sometimes you want to go where everybody knows your name." That is Squirrel Hill. It is the sort of place where you would want to live, because it is a place where your soul would want to live.

And then, of course, Tree of Life Synagogue itself — a place, like many of its neighbors, that has nurtured the spirits of generations of Pittsburgh Jews.

Second, sacred times. The attack happened on Shabbat. If the synagogue is where Jews are, then Shabbat is when Jews are.

No surprise, as well; some of the most prodigious Jew-haters in history deliberately chose Jewish sacred days as the days for attack — the Nazis, who chose Jewish holidays for aktionen; the Arabs, who attacked Israel on Yom Kippur; Palestinian terrorists, who attacked a seder at the Park Hotel in Netanya.

Third, sacred values. The gunman attacked Tree of Life Synagogue's building for the institution's linkage to HIAS. HIAS began its noble history by taking care of Jewish immigrants; it continues that sacred mission by taking care of all immigrants and refugees.

The shooter hates immigrants. Therefore, he hates HIAS. Therefore, he hates the Jews who have supported HIAS. He hates the Jews because of our values. He hates the Jews because we are the descendants of Abraham and Sarah, who kept their desert tent open on all sides.

What do we do? We double down. We lean in. We affirm our values. We affirm the centrality of the synagogue in the lives of Jews. Rather than be afraid of bringing ourselves and our children to synagogue, let us triple our efforts to do so. Maintain your membership in the Jewish community. Your presence is a fist that you shake in the face of the haters.

And, finally: Do not despair. We have many friends.

My dear friend, the Rev. Richard Burnett of Trinity Episcopal Church in Columbus, Ohio told me that his church would be ringing its bells this morning — eleven times: *Once, for each victim.*

I like bells. But, I also like shofars. It is time for us to blow the shofar, again — as a sign of mourning, and of rage, and of warning. We blow the shofar of rage and of warning — against the American cult of death, the fundamentalism of "gunolatry," that refuses to compromise one inch, and one drop of blood, in order to make this nation safer.

The late David Bowie got it right:

"This is not America."

A portion of the proceeds from this book will support efforts to end the American Gun Violence epidemic.

Rabbi Menachem Creditor is the Pearl and Ira Meyer Scholar in Residence of UJA-Federation New York and the founder of Rabbis Against Gun Violence.

Named by Newsweek as one of the 50 most influential rabbis in America, his song, *Olam Chesed Yibaneh/Build this World from Love*, has become an anthem of hope around the world. He has authored 17 books and released 6 albums of original music. Rabbi Creditor has been a featured contributor to media outlets including The Times of Israel, the Huffington Post, and The Daily Forward.

A frequent speaker on Jewish Leadership and Literacy in communities around the United States and Israel, he served for more than a decade as spiritual leader of Congregation Netivot Shalom in Berkeley, California, a Trustee of American Jewish World Service, co-chair of Shalom Bayit, the One America Movement and sits on the Social Justice Commission of the Rabbinical Assembly.

Find out more at menachemcreditor.net